GREAT PR⭘FIT IDEAS

BOOK OF BUSINESS IDEAS

VOLUME 6 (501-600)

100
IDEAS

Great Profit Ideas is a series of cost reducing business ideas created to boost your bottom line. Use this book of ideas and actions to cut costs, improve margins, and increase sales.

GREAT PR☯FIT IDEAS

BOOK OF BUSINESS IDEAS

VOLUME 6 (501-600)

100
IDEAS

By

Donald S. Sylvester

ISBN: 978-1-71681-389-4

How To Effectively Use This Book
To Boost Your Bottom Line

This collection of 100 (501 to 600) brief, randomly written and entered but highly effective business ideas and concepts was assembled for any business reader to use as a reference tool. When searching for ideas, he can turn to any page in the book and pick an easy action to implement, decision to make or idea to try out within any company. The ideas were deliberately written in brief to get to the point for the reader so he can scan several ideas and get to something he likes quickly.

Try One Every Day: Every idea will either directly or indirectly cut costs, improve margins, or increase sales, all of which boost the bottom line of any company.

The reader can pick out any one and try it out or scan the entire book and note the ones liked and write them down or their page numbers on the Favorites Lists featured at the end of the book.

Log Your Favorites In The Back Of The Book: One other idea is for the reader to note his favorite ideas in the back and then forward the book to other managers and supervisors to read or scan and enter their favorites also.

Implement One Every Day: Regardless of the method that is used, read the ideas, choose the ones you like and want to try and go put them into action and increase your company's bottom line.

Consider An Incentive Program For Employees' Ideas: Add to your own list by adding some awards for good employee ideas. It will boost morale and encourage employee innovation.

Measure Your Success: If one idea does not work, select another, and try it. Go pick an idea to start, watch and measure the favorable results and see your company make more money.

About The Author and This Book

Donald Sylvester has over 40 years of experience working as a controller and CFO for several companies located in the U.S. and Canada. Those positions all provided great learning experience and spanned several varied industries (i.e. automotive parts, book manufacturing, oil and gas supplies, parts and equipment, real estate development and hazardous waste service industries).

With this experience gained in heavy manufacturing, machining, construction (project management), importing, distribution and real estate development, Donald witnessed a number of companies improve the bottom line quickly. He thought one main reason for the continual profit improvement of these totally independent but successful business stories stemmed from one simple attribute — "Ask questions continually, be quiet and listen."

His daughter, Aura, while she was attending college classes, asked him to begin writing brief business ideas so she could learn some of the issues that face business owners every day.

The one thing she insisted upon was getting to the point and creating a list of questions or ideas so the reader could understand the benefit quickly.

Donald wrote these ideas not only for Aura to learn but to be designed for businesspeople to use on their jobs. This accumulation of actions and ideas were created to simply give the reader options to choose from a number of business categories (i.e. accounts payable, production, sales, purchasing, collections, cost reductions).

As a reader, you can pick one or more and take action.

Whatever you do, remember not to ask the questions only once. Ask questions of everyone on all management levels continuously. If you try ten suggestions but only one is profitable, it will still be worth your time. Pick out those questions or ideas you like. Change them to meet the needs of your company. Use them regularly and this author knows you will boost your bottom line.

Table Of Ideas By Business Area

BUSINESS AREA	IDEAS BY NUMBER
Accounts Payable – AP Discounts, Invoice Review, AP Statement Review, Vendor Corrections, Catching Invoicing Errors, Get invoices For Variable Auto-Debited Charges	502, 503, 504, 506, 511, 555, 573
Accounts Payable – Vendor Auto-Debit Payments, Verify Rental Unit Usage Before Paying, Do Not Issue AP Checks Without Addresses, Do Lay Off Employees Then Hire Then Thru AP	539, 552, 578, 577
Accounts Receivable – Collections, Monitoring New Orders To Help Collections, Apply Cash Daily to Discover Problems, Send Proofs Of Delivery With All Invoices	523, 553, 596
Accounts Receivable – Granting Credit, Credit Insurance, Give Favorable Credit References To Good-Paying Customers	540, 561

Table Of Ideas By Business Area

BUSINESS AREA	IDEAS BY NUMBER
Administration – Receptionist, Incoming Mail	501, 510, 513, 514
Billings – Researching New Customers, Check These Items Before First Invoice For New Customers, Billing Inventory Before Receiving Goods, Bill On Online Portals ASAP, Send Proofs of Delivery With All Invoices	547, 554, 555, 588, 596
Cost Reductions – Early CPA Audit, Limit Postage Meter Use, Rent Older Units, Cleaning Personnel Feedback, Do Not Allow Non-Purchasing Employees To Buy, Using NAICS Codes To Find Alternative Material Vendors, Are We Wasting Packaging Materials,	530, 531, 535, 537, 559, 560, 566
CPA Firms – Save Audit Fees – Plan Early	530
Credit Card – Offer Small Discount To Check Photo ID To Cut Credit Card Theft	599

Table Of Ideas By Business Area

BUSINESS AREA	IDEAS BY NUMBER
Drivers – Driver Training And Sales Training, Website Access To Vehicle Insurance Certificates, Daily Checklist To Inspect The Truck, Notify Customers Of Late Deliveries	507, 551, 555, 557
Employees – Getting Feedback, Acknowledge Work Anniversaries, Safe Driving Bonuses	525, 545
Employees – Training And Overtime	562
Finance – Loan Payment Comparisons, Diverse Industries For Inventory (Loans), Rebid Offered Financing Bids From Your Vendors	509, 541, 591
Financial Statements – How Long To Issue Financial Statements?	583

Table Of Ideas By Business Area

BUSINESS AREA	IDEAS BY NUMBER
Freight – Internal Freight Analysis, Annual Inspections And Repairs, Safe Driving Bonuses, Daily Checklist To Inspect Company Truck, Require Signed BOLs From Drivers, Ask Truck Drivers What Can Be Improved, Offer To Open Early For Freight Discount	532. 533, 545, 555, 587, 588, 590, 598
Insurance – Cut Cost By Limiting Items Insured, Cut Coverage To Liability	521, 524
Insurance – Insurance Broker Discounts For Employees' Insurance	543
Insurance – Vehicle Insurance, Annual Evidence Of Damage And Mileage, Safe Driving Bonus Program, Website Insurance Certificates	544, 545, 551
Inventory – Ability To Resell	541

Table Of Ideas By Business Area

BUSINESS AREA	IDEAS BY NUMBER
Inventory – Ongoing Cycle Count Program, Review Inventory Report For Errors	538, 555
IT – Temporary Internet Access For Visitors	550
Legal – Clearing Copier Memory /Disk Images, Analyzing New Purchase Orders, Researching New Companies In State Corporation Engines	508, 546, 547
Marketing – Improving Customer Service, Mark Your Building With Your Physical Address, Publish List Of All Businesses Within Zip Code	548, 545, 597
Marketing – Analyzing Other Products Based Upon Company Assets, Buy From Competitors To See What You Need To Do	519, 558

Table Of Ideas By Business Area

BUSINESS AREA	IDEAS BY NUMBER
Marketing – Website, Teach Customers To Make Website Relevant, How Long To Change Screens On The Company Website?	529, 582
Payroll – Vendor Discount Employee Benefits, Training New Hires And Overtime, Payroll Deducted Two Days Before Pay Date, Always Pay Employees On Time, Pay An Outside Firm To Do Payroll	542, 543, 562 .580, 581, 592
Productivity – Ask Machine Operators What Is Wrong With Programming	565
Purchasing – Buying From Neighbors, Altering Bid Submission Personnel, Feedback From Contractors (Cleaning), Using NAICS Codes To Find Alternative Vendor Sources, Email At Holidays To Reveal All Other Buyers, Publish List Of All Businesses Within Your Zip Code	515, 516, 518, 537, 560, 579, 597

Table Of Ideas By Business Area

BUSINESS AREA	IDEAS BY NUMBER
Purchasing – Employee Vendor Discounts (Benefits), Analyzing New Purchase Orders, Do Not Allow Non-Purchasing Personnel To Buy, For Customers With No Pos, Issue Back Full Emails And Ask For Acceptance	542, 546, 559, 576
Receiving – No Receiving Reports For Rental Units, Inventory Report Error When Billings Precedes Receiving Parts, Receiving Parts On Correct Dates	552, 555
Sales – Getting Feedback, Sales Personnel Dropping Off Small Shipments, Tell Customers When Product Shipments Will Arrive	527, 564, 574
Sales – Selling To Neighbors, Selling To New Customers	515, 517, 547

Table Of Ideas By Business Area

BUSINESS AREA	IDEAS BY NUMBER
Sales – Increasing Sales / Broadening Sales Base, Notifying Customers Of Late Shipments, Expand Sales – Offer Goods & Services Outside The Company Catalog	520, 557,600
Sales – Increasing Customer Service, Update Customers On Late Orders, Teach Customers Every Day, Apply Cash Daily To Discover Customer Disputes, Buy From Competitors To See What You Are Missing, Give Favorable Credit References For Your Better-Paying Customers – Let Them Know It, Bill Expediting Fees For Faster Delivery, Send List Of All Businesses Within Your Zip Code	526, 528, 548, 550, 553, 558, 561, 586, 597
Sales – Training Sales Personnel Key Points To Win Contracts, Arrange Sales Visits Within Zip Codes	534, 563

Table Of Ideas By Business Area

BUSINESS AREA	IDEAS BY NUMBER
Sales – Travel Expenses / Rent Older Vehicles, No Insurance On Rental Units,	535, 536
Shipping – Are We Wasting Packaging Materials, Post TV Screen Showing Late Jobs In Shipping, Pay Shipping Bonuses To Cut Late Shipments	566, 584, 585
Taxes – Property Taxes / Filing Renditions, After Land/Building Purchase Check Property Tax Records Online For Errors, Pay Taxes At Post Office On Time Certified Mail For Proof	512, 593, 594
Training – Using NAICS Codes To Find Alternative Vendors (Training Purchasing Agents)	560
Vehicles – Measuring Mileage	544
Vendors – Copier Vendor	508

501. **Legal Protection: Date Stamp All Incoming Mail /Email:** When receiving, opening mail and or printing incoming email, use a date stamp to indicate when your company received these documents for future reference (i.e. invoices, statements, legal notices, registrations, tax bills, garnishments, court orders, late notices etc.). For example: Your accounting system will show the invoice from your vendor dated January 10th that was not physically received until January 21st when the postman brought it to the office. You need to date stamp mail if questioned later by the sender.

502. **Ask Vendors For Statements At Month End**: To ensure you have received all invoices for a closing period, ask your key vendors to forward a complete month end statement to your attention so you can be certain all invoices were received. This is very necessary when a company bills on a

time and material basis (labor hours billed at a higher flat rate and purchased materials marked up 10 to 20%. Under this billing agreement, vendor invoices become important at that point because without an invoice, your company misses a profit markup on the month-end billings to the customer. You also want to ensure you have received and booked all the costs associated with the fiscal month.

503. **Call And Ask To Take AP Discounts After The Allowed Period Has Lapsed**: It is worth calling the customer and asking about taking the offered discount even if the period has passed. Most of the time, the customer wants the money and will not risk the vendor not paying on the 15th day on 2% 10, Net 30. Most customers want the money even if the vendor misses the payment deadline.

504. **Do Not Sign AP Checks Without Reviewing The Invoices Being Paid:** Normally accounts payable checks need to be signed after they are printed and cut.

They are normally manually signed by a supervisor or by two authorized employees if certain dollar limits are exceeded. The responsibility of the signer is not to just sign the checks but also to do a final check to compare the paid amount of the check to the invoice backup. The invoices being paid are detailed on the check remittance advice (attachment detailing backup on the check) with the originals attached to offer a final outside review.

505. **Reject Vendor Invoices With Sales Taxes Incorrectly Charged**: When reviewing incoming vendor invoices every day, check to ensure sales taxes are not charged if the purchase is exempt. If the manufacturing company receives an invoice for the purchase of materials used in manufacturing for example that has sales tax charged incorrectly, reject the invoice upfront. Send the vendor the company's sales tax exemption certificate for that state where the sale occurred and ask for a corrected invoice. Do not accept incorrect

invoices on a promise to receive a credit in the future because it is too easy to forget and complicates AP records for any sales tax audits. Insist that you receive a corrected invoice upfront from the vendor.

506. **Find Money: Ask For Vendor Statements To Find Their Credits:** Ask vendors on a regular basis for a statement of invoices because sometimes you will find unused credits for which you are unaware. Most vendors will not make a call to you to tell you to take your available credits so ask for regular statements to find them. Vendors will issue credits to their customers but not send them out repeatedly like they do past due invoices, thus, asking for statements sometimes will reveal unused credits they issued which the company needs to use and deduct on the next vendor check cut.

507. **Instruct Drivers To Clarify Receiving Signatures At The Point Of Delivery:** When your driver delivers a load to the customer's facility, before leaving he

normally asks the customer's representative to sign for the delivery. To avoid questions or doubts about the authenticity of the signature, clarify who signed the bill of lading (BOL) in behalf of the customer by writing the signer's name when it is illegible. Tell your driver if he cannot read the signature once written, to ask the person how they spell their last name. Ask your driver to then handwrite that printed name on the bill of lading below the illegible signature before leaving. This will help to eliminate arguments from the customer stating they do not recognize the receiver's signature.

508. **Ask Copier Representative To Clear All Copy Machine Disc Memories**: Some copier machines contain a computer disc inside that is scanning and retaining copies of all scanned documents sent or received by those who operated the machine in the past. This memory may go back a couple of months or several years depending upon the copier. To protect the company, ask the

copier representative how to have this memory cleaned and deleted to protect the company renting the machine. The images could be personal documents, employee records with social security, birth records and other private details that were not meant to be recorded in anyway or legal documents that could be ordered taken and retained by a court order.

509. **Compare Real Estate Loan Payment Amounts Versus Only Interest Rate Percentages:** When comparing loans, especially those for financing or refinancing real estate, ask to see the monthly payments. See if the calculations are based upon a commercial loan calculation (principle divided by number of months plus accrued monthly interest resulting in variable monthly amounts, high to low) or an amortized loan (all loan amounts equal amount over life of loan). The longer the loan, the greater the cash difference between the two regardless of the interest rate. If the buyer wants to

payoff principle as quickly as possible, he will choose the commercial loan. If the buyer wants to minimize the monthly cash payment, he will desire the amortized loan (lower initial payment).

510. **Mark Incorrect Personal Or Business Mail And "Return To Sender":** When receiving mail addressed to the wrong address or to a tenant no longer located at the company address, mark the tenant "No Longer Here" and then circle the return address and mark the piece of mail "Return To Sender". Do not open this mail addressed to another party. Return it through your mailman. Marking this mail will help to force the sending company to correct its records and help relieve the company of any complaints about non-delivered mail from ex-tenants (especially late tax notices, legal notices from local and federal courts). Return it with the outgoing mail and force the post office to legally return it to the mailer.

511. **Correct Company Addresses On All Incoming Invoices And Email:** Notice any incorrect company addresses on incoming mail and email and notify the companies their records are incorrect. Notify them of your correct physical address. It is your company's responsibility to notify the vendor of an incorrect address. Emailed invoices should be corrected also in the event the vendor is attempting to contact the company physically with direct mail or to make a visit.

512. **Cut Property Taxes – Choose Wisely For Assigned Vehicle Locations For Filing Property Tax Renditions:** The company may own many vehicles and operate several physical locations in different counties throughout the state. Since the vehicles are constantly moving from location to location, when filing the rendition (required filing of declared value of assets once per year), choose the least expensive location to declare the vehicles

for property taxes since county taxes vary by appraisal district.

513. **Instruct Receptionist To Forward Calls To A Knowledgeable Backup:** When the receptionist receives a call he or she does not know how to handle, always have someone knowledgeable assigned who will take the call. For example, when a lawyer representing an ex-employee calls, someone who understands that a legal claim may be involved knows that the lawyer on the telephone will need to talk to the company's lawyer or law firm. If the caller is a vendor who has received a check sent to the wrong party by the AP department, someone needs to take the call and then possibly stop payment on the check. If the incoming call has to do with bank account problems, someone in accounting needs to correct the bank problem (check, deposit slip error, bank account transfer problem). Other issues that come up may include examples such as these: 1.) sales tax audits, 2.) law

enforcement officers calling about a company vehicle complaint or driver complaint, 3.) a person calling to claim a cracked windshield caused by the company truck, 4.) a caller seeking child support from a current employee or, 5.) a vendor calling and claiming damage incurred from a visiting company truck.

514. **Use A 9 Digit Zip Code On All Company Mail:** To speed up mail delivery to your customers and vendors, use their entire 9-digit zip code. Using the extra four digits defines mailing routes and helps to obtain bulk mailing discounts as well as increases the chance that it will make it to the correct address on time.

515. **Make A List For Purchasing And Sales Of All Neighbor Businesses And What They Sell:** Have someone in the company's inside sales or marketing departments call all of the neighboring companies within two or three blocks and find out what they make, service or resell. Tell them you are making a list of the local

businesses in your area. Record their contact information for sales and for purchasing and create a list for your sales personnel to hand out to each as they visit them. Give it to your neighbors and ask that they consider buying from your firm given that you can sell to them most likely with free freight and discounted prices since they are across the street. Pass out the list to both purchasing agents and inside sales personnel to all the neighbors.

516. **Use Neighborhood Business List To Buy From Neighbors**: Ask purchasing what they can buy from neighbors from the Neighborhood Business List created by marketing. Go through the list of goods and services and ask for quotes from your neighbors. Consider freight savings and the fact you may not need to buy so much because these suppliers are nearby. It is especially important to consider buying from a neighbor if they turn into a customer.

517. **Use Neighborhood Business List To Sell To Neighbors**: Ask the sales personnel to take the Neighborhood Business List and see what neighbors may be potential buyers. Offer a preferential price schedule and no freight costs to boost interest. Customers across the street are the easiest customers to service and ship to (via forklift if down the street for examples). Find out if any are sister divisions of current companies and offer corporate discounts to both if both buy from your company.

518. **Encourage More Bidders: Alter Where Incoming Vendor Bids Are Submitted:** Make sure all incoming bids from vendors into the purchasing department are sent to alternating personnel. Change the receiving person regularly. This will put pressure on bidders to turn in their best bid, thwart friendships between vendors and purchasing agents and invite more bidders to come to the company knowing the

selection process is open, impartial, and conducted fairly and openly.

519. **Given Company Assets, Locations And Capabilities, Make A List Of What <u>Other</u> Products Can Be Sold:** Instead of always selling within the same industry or selling only the same products, analyze what other products can be made and what other industries the company can attempt to enter. If the company has large tanks for blending drilling liquids, are those tanks capable of blending nearly any other type of chemical liquid? If the company makes and sells ice cream, is it capable of making other food products (given its outlets, distributors, and current customers)?

520. **Ask Your Sales Personnel Their Favorite Top Five Customers, Then Give Them Similar Lists Of Sales Leads:** Ask your sales personnel the names of their top five customers (you choose the number). Prepare for those sales personnel a list of all other potential customers in their territory with the same categorization. Get

this listing by using those original customers' SIC codes as a base to look up other potential customers with the same code located in the defined sales territory. Using a free local library card, look up other SIC code related companies within a 50, 100, 250 or 500 mile radius (you pick the miles) or a specific metro area, or a state, or a city. The printouts that are available include company names, addresses, telephone numbers, fax numbers, contact names, estimated sales size, and many more fields of data. Once these reports are run for the salesperson, that will cause future requests, especially if they derive commissions out of those successful sales calls from those lists. Continually search the database for current customers' SIC codes to expand the search and increase the number of potential sales leads for your salespeople.

521. **Cut Insurance Premiums: Do Not Insure Older Equipment:** If the company has older equipment with low or minimal

market value, exclude it from the equipment list for insurance purposes. The age you select to delete the equipment from your list depends upon your company type. For example, most pickup trucks after 10 years old are fully depreciated, easily traded in but by themselves are not worth a lot. Some pieces of equipment in seven or eight years are fully depreciated and need to be replaced by newer equipment because of their restricted productivity, but they do not necessarily need to be insured. Cut the premium and save it because the market value of the lost piece of equipment is probably low anyway. Save the insurance premium cost and eliminate equipment on future policies that pass an established company age limit.

522. **Cut Insurance Premiums: On Older Vehicles, Carry Only Liability Insurance:** When renewing insurance premiums for the company, choose an age and change full coverage premium to liability only to cut the insurance cost.

Vehicles older than say ten years probably do not have a large market value so cut the cost of insuring them. Save on the insurance premium by reducing the coverage down to only the minimum liability coverage, especially on older vehicles.

523. **Cut Insurance Premiums: Increase Deductibles For Accident Claims:** Increase the deductibles on the company insurance policy to cut the annual premiums, especially if your company has a good prior safety record with few accidents. This insurance policy savings also can be used to pay drivers for errorless spot-free driving records. Make it worthwhile financially for your drivers never to cause an accident or receive a ticket.

524. **Allow The AR Collections Agent To See All New Incoming Purchase Orders To Help Collect Past Dues:** Let the collection agents see all new incoming purchase orders to catch new orders from past due

clients. The ideal situation would be to let them authorize the orders first before confirming the orders as is. The collection agent may notify the customer's purchasing agent that the company is waiting on payment for past due and any help from his department would be appreciated. If this is not desired, ask the order takers to contact the buyer and tell him of the late charges. Whoever deals with the buyer needs to either tell him the order will be fulfilled or not (depending upon the age and size of the current past due invoices.)

525. **Acknowledge Employee Work Anniversaries:** Make sure to acknowledge employee work anniversaries. Make a list in chronological order for the year of all anniversaries (hire dates or last review and increase dates). Even if you do not award an employee an increase, have the meeting about his or her progress in the position, list what needs to be improved or compliment the progress made and then if earned, make an attempt if financially possible, to give

the employee an increase. If the company is not financially able to give him an increase, give him some idea when that time is over so he knows that he will be awarded at some time. It is bad not to mention anything to the employees and potentially make them worry about whether they are doing a bad job or why they did not get an increase for the year.

526. **Talk To Customers With Late Open Orders Not Yet Shipped And Give Them An Estimate:** Do not wait for the buyer to call the company wondering why their shipment was not shipped. Assign someone in sales or marketing to review all the late shipments, obtain a best estimated new date of shipment, then call the customer to let them know it is indeed going to be shipped. Make sure to supply them the date when it should be on a truck on the way to their designated facility. Offer to personally call them the day their late order ships if they need to be notified. Make sure they are notified and not ignored.

527. Ask Your Company's Outside Independent Sales Agents What Is Wrong With Your Company: Ask your outside sales agents who draw a commission each month what is wrong with your company. They are limited on what they earn from you because of your failings, deficiencies, discrepancies, lousy customer service, slow response time or even worse, an unresponsive inside sales department. Agents who feel cheated out of commissions and monthly earned fees will certainly tell you what is wrong and what needs to be improved. They do not have anything to lose except more commissions. Yes, they will certainly tell you.

528. Tell Your Customers How To Save Money Regardless Of The Product Or Service You Offer: Try to make a list of methods your customers can save money when they do business with your company. **Insurance:** For insurance brokers, list out for the customer, higher deductible policies, the elimination of certain assets not worth insuring, alternative methods for insuring property that carry lower premiums, consideration of lower total insurance coverages or lower limits on what will be paid out. **Materials Supplier**: List for customers the price breaks available on certain volume purchases, reduction in cost with customer pickup, price breaks on various container sizes (bigger containers, cheaper unit costs), cheaper grade material alternatives for sale or lower priced damaged goods that may be applicable for the specific customers' application. **Hair Salon:** Give a discount to those who come on the known 'slow' days of the week for that salon. **Grocery Store**: Display all the items on sale for the week at the front of the store before entering customers start shopping (or mark them clearly in the aisleways) plus offer free recipes to prepare from the items that are on sale. **Ice Cream Store:** Offer a cheaper price for the flavor few customers bought for the week (overstocked supply available).

529. **Teach Customers How To Do Something On Your Company Website To Make It Relevant:** Most company websites are poorly designed and offer no constructive information to customers. To change this, feature some type of new instructions every week. **Paint Stores:** Detail step by step how homeowners can finish the walls in their homes first, apply a coat of stain coat for water stains, then how to apply paint over that preapplication, how long to wait and how long to stay out of the room for the odor. **Grocery Stores:** These stores feature items on sale and recipes to use the food that they sell. **Shoe Stores:** Feature short videos how to clean shoes and apply a polish or wax and buff finish. **Pharmacy:** How to take medicine and what to do for certain side effects or sickness. How to contact the pharmacist for suggestions on reactions or how to contact insurance companies to check on coverage or reimbursement. **Makeup Companies:** How to properly apply their firm's makeup and what to use to remove it easily. **Tool**

Companies: Videos on how to effectively and safely use any tool the company sells. **Veterinarians:** Videos to show pet owners how to check for ticks, check for injuries or sores, check the pet's teeth, notice behaviors or food reactions, etc. **Tax Preparers:** Short videos of checklists of various costs, receipts, and other financial costs to consider and document to save the maximum of amount of local, state, and federal income taxes. **CPA Firms**: Checklists of items that can be prepared ahead of schedule and emailed in to speed up the required field work and hopefully reduce the overall audit fee.

530. **Schedule Your Audit Before Fiscal Yearend And Ask For Audit Cutting Ideas:** In order to save money and cut cost, ask your CPA firm to list all the tasks that can be done prior yearend closing. Their time gets busy after the first of the year with audits and tax schedule preparation so doing anything prior to yearend when they are not as busy should help cut the cost.

531. **Enter A Required Code First Before Accessing Use Of Your Postage Meter:** Do not allow everyone access to your postage meter. Acquire a model which allows the designated user to set up a code that must be entered first before applying postage to company letters and envelopes. Enforce the required code to a limited number of people allowed to charge postage to minimize postage theft.

532. **Measure Productivity Of Your Company Trucks**: What percentage of miles driven per month earned a profit: 1.) delivering goods to a customer or a sale, 2.) picking up materials at a freight free cost, lower cost, 3.) earning paid mileage from third parties on long return trips hired through a freight internet site?   Assign the driver to track all miles driven per month and how those trips earned money for the company (sales, freight reduced costs for purchases, hired mileage for return trips for unbusy days). When he exceeds a certain percentage (i.e. 75% or 80% of the

budgeted hours for the month = 22 workdays x 8 hours per day = 176 total hours x 75% =132 billable/ earning hours per month), pay him a bonus. Make sure the higher the percentage, the more money he can make. This makes the driver finish loads on time, offer to pick up loads on the drive home trip and check back with the home office frequently to find out his next assignment in order to drive up his productivity percentage.

533. **Coordinate All Vehicle Inspections With Company Sanctioned Dealer Service Center**:   Force all company vehicles to go through the company selected service dealer who performs all the regular scheduled maintenance. His contract will require any work done to be at lower company negotiated rates. When he finds problems with the vehicles during the required annual inspections, he will repair the vehicles at the negotiated lower service rates at the same time reporting conditions

of the company vehicles (abuse, wrecks, damage, etc.).

534. **Find Out The Most Important Elements Of Making Your Company's Sales Pitch To New Customers**: Ask all of your sales people what are the subjects/issues/'hot buttons' that must be mentioned and discussed when getting potential customers interested in making a purchase or signing an agreement with the company for making a sale. The sales personnel who sell everyday know what key issues are the most important because they have seen them work. Ask all your salespeople to write down and submit their terms or ideas and make a complete list for everyone to use and refer to. Some examples may include. 1.) free freight, 2.) free customer service for 90 days after contract date, 3.) one no-cost day of employee training on customer's site, 4.) vendor has the available capacity to triple manufacturing within six months if requested by the customer, 5.) deliver in six different size containers

(6,000 gallon tankers, 290 gallon totes, 55 gallon drums, 30 gal containers, 1 gallon jugs, or 12 oz squeeze bottles), 6.) customer may inspect the manufacturing plant 24/7 with no notice, 7.) rejected parts come back with 125% return price which includes rejection fees paid to the customer to have to handle bad materials shipped by the vendor, 8.) certificate of insurance issued with $10M total liability and the customer as a 'named payee' on the policy, 9.) product comes in five colors, three sizes, and reusable containers. 10.) Order turnaround is less than 24 hours. Whatever those key issues are in your industry to be successful, write them down. Summarize them in one sales 'checklist' to give to everyone in sales and in the future. Date the listing because requirements and needs change in the marketplace. Update the list as needed as the market changes and customers' demands change.

535. **Save Money On Company Leased Vehicles – Rent Older Units:** When

leasing vehicles, ask to see the prices of any older models carried in stock (they should be leased more cheaply because most companies want newer models). Instruct purchasing personnel to obtain quotes for older vehicles (three to five years old) to save leasing costs.

536. **Do Not Allow Rental Companies To Charge For Insurance – Buy Your Own Coverage:** When renting or leasing vehicles or trucks, do not allow the rental company to provide and charge you insurance. Get your own insurance broker or insurance company to cover the vehicle. It will be far cheaper and will not contain as high a markup as through the rental company. You have the power of a larger internal insurance contract so use it and do not allow your employees to let the rental company charge insurance.

537. **Ask Cleaning Personnel To Leave A Checklist Of Problems Noted**: Ask the cleaning personnel who clean the company offices, warehouses, and any company

facilities to complete a checklist of issues noted during their weekly visit. Include in the checklist items such as 1.) urinals leaking, 2.) toilets leaking or running occasionally, 3.) evidence of any electrical sparking or black soot, 4.) any paint stained from water damage, 5.) evidence of water leakage from the roof, 6.) any unusual cars or trucks sitting in the parking lot during the cleaning visit, 7.) any product or odd items seen in the trash or noticeably tossed out in trash bags, 8.) problems locking doors or loose equipment (not secured), 9.) anything unusual noticed from week to week. Any observations that can be solicited from the cleaning people will help to indicate problems they noticed. Ask that they include it daily or at least weekly along with their invoice.

538. **Benefit From An On-Going Cycle-Counting Program Covering All Inventory Every 30, 60 or 90 Days**: Most companies with a sizeable stock will have an on-going cycle count program where a

knowledgeable crew counts a selected portion of inventory every day for the company. Those members are assigned chunks of the inventory by location code and stock number and understand the process how to adjust for receipts and shipments to make correct adjustments constantly in the inventory system every day. Normally they will count critical parts far more often than slow moving stock. After a period of methodical counting, they will normally cover everything in inventory each one, two or three months (depending upon the demands and turnover of the stock). When they perform their cycle count, they will enter verification dates when the counts were verified which helps planners and inside sales personnel feel more comfortable acknowledging requested products for customers that are known to be 'in stock' per the cycle-count date.

539. **Make A Chronological List Of All Automatic Authorized Debits To Company Bank Accounts:** Many

companies opt into allowing ongoing vendors to debit their checking accounts. This includes charges for property rents, vehicle rents, electric, gas and telephone bills and nearly any other ongoing monthly charge that the company will allow to be debited. List these out chronologically and make sure there is a debit limit established for every automatic payment. For example, allow up to $500 to be charged for an electric bill so the bill of $849 will be refused (at least until the bill can be reviewed and approved).

540. **Clear Credit Insurance Before Extending Sizeable Credit To A New Unknown Customer**: You may be able to call and ask any of the 50+ large credit insurance companies whether they issue policies on a new proposed customer name your sales personnel brought to the company. Normally they want to sell you an insurance policy so you can buy the insurance in the event of the customer's default but knowing they feel comfortable

enough to issue the policy may be good enough without buying it. You can contact your bank also and ask your relationship manager whether they know anything about this potential customer.

541. **Maximize Inventory Advances On Bank Loans – List The Multiple Industries Where It Can Be Sold**: When your company is looking for a bank loan (asset based loan), remember that in order to get loan coverage for inventory, the bank needs to feel comfortable that they will have no problem calling and selling your remaining inventory stock. Explain to the bank field audit what your inventory is and what other industries uses these items and for what purpose. If you do not know the other uses in the market for the stock you purchase, call the sales representative that sells to your firm and ask for a list of the types of companies that buy the same inventory and ask the multiple purposes that it has. This will enable you to borrow a higher percentage against inventory because it will

alleviate fears of the bank that in the event your firm goes bankrupt, the bank has multiple places to sell off the remaining inventory.

542. **Instruct Purchasing To Request Vendors To Offer Discounts To The Company Employees**:   When negotiating with vendors, when it is appropriate, ask that they offer discounts to the company employees. Most vendors will do so just to get more business and increase their chances of winning more work contracts. Ask that they provide a poster that can be hung in the company's facilities for all employees to see. Include a small flyer in the employees' paychecks to let them know of further additional 'benefits' of working for the company.

543. **Ask Company's Insurance Broker For Possible Employee Home And Auto Insurance Discounts:**   Ask the insurance broker for the company if he can offer any type of discount for auto and home insurance for company employees. He may

not be able to but referral companies, insurance connections and personal insurance agencies he is connected to may be able to help. Any reduction company employees can get from obtaining a free quote through your company insurance broker is perceived as another benefit working for the company.

544. **Evidence Of Low Mileage May Cut Insurance Costs:** Once a year, request pictures of all the assigned vehicles' odometer readings. This will help to prove to insurers the low mileage on some of the vehicles thus helping to drive down the quotes for car and truck insurance, especially for the second reading one year later. A good time to probably do it is when the notice of registration comes due. Once notified by your state that a vehicle has an annual registration coming due, request the driver to submit a picture of the vehicle (evidence of good shape or signs of damage not yet reported) along with a picture of the odometer reading. At that

point, the company can argue with the insurance company or broker to go look for lower rates if the mileage on the vehicle has been low for the previous year (lower mileage, less risk, lower premium).

545. **Instruct Safe Company Drivers Formally How To Apply For Driving Bonuses:** Pay your drivers not to have accidents and to drive safely avoiding any traffic tickets. Formalize a program designed to reward their good performance which also will cut insurance premiums. That program will pay them once they pass a quarter, six months or a year without accidents and tickets (you decide the time periods). Tell the drivers in the program after passing a bonus program milestone to request the logistics department to run their new driving record (to ensure no tickets given in the past year which then can be supplied to bidding insurance companies). Then instruct the drivers to take pictures of their truck showing no current damage and of the truck's current odometer reading. After that

is completed, ask them to turn in the paperwork to be rewarded with their bonus check. To ensure the success of the program, pay them often and do not hesitate or make them wait when they have done a good job. Take pictures of the best drivers and post them on your website to show customers you value safety and will reward it handsomely.

546. **Review 1st Purchase Orders From New Customers Extensively Before Acceptance**: When receiving a new purchase order from a new company, take the time to analyze all the data presented. Find out the billing address, physical address for delivery. Is the physical address where the company product is to be delivered a customer's owned facility or is this an address of the customer (drop shipment)? If it is a drop shipment, who needs to sign the bill of lading and what is the procedure if different than that of delivering to them at their own location? What are the payment terms and if missing,

refer to any master service agreement or previously signed contract?   Are pricing and accepted quantity levels correct? Can your company overbill the quantity (i.e. 10% more, 20% more) or will it be rejected? Or missing? What are the freight terms? Note the correct company name, company address, telephone number, fax number and any website address on the purchase order and put them into the company database along with the name and phone number of the person who will be paying this first invoice. If he or she is noted, enter the assigned purchasing agent who initiated the order.

547. **Look Up New Customers Online In Each State's Corporation Search Engine:** Before setting up new customers in the company database, search for their name to be registered within the state of their physical address. Type in "Georgia Corporation Search" or "Texas Corporation Search". Make sure it is the state's website and not a paid website. If the customer's

name cannot be found, call them, and ask what company name they used to get set up within the state to do business. They must be listed to do business in the state where they are located. Most states will also note if they are behind on paying taxes or have not filed tax returns, or if they closed recently. Notice of the address they used to be notified of any problems by the state and who their registered agent is (if not themselves). Most smaller companies will not pay for a registered agent and will list the owner as the registered agent (which helps identify who to sue during collection efforts).

548. **Open, Take Calls And Ship Orders When Your Customers Are Working**: If your company is trying to sell to all parts of the country, it will need to answer telephone calls for time zones depending upon the level of competition. If your product is unique and not carried by anyone else, it will be irrelevant since customers must wait for you to open to call your firm.

If you are in a competitive market with multiple customer options, then you must adjust to meet the demands of the market. If a customer can easily call and reach a competitor while you are still closed, you are most likely losing sales. Many buyers have many products and services to buy so they will not call your company repeatedly if there is a competitor available to answer questions, take orders and ship the products with one telephone call. You may believe that all customers want to buy online but most have questions that they need to discuss with a voice on the telephone before ordering. That voice answers questions, clarifies issues and reassures them before they place an order. Open early for the market you serve.

549. **Take An Order On The Telephone From A Customer – Do Not Send Them To Your Website**:   If you have a customer on the telephone and he is happy with all of the answers to his questions, offer to take his order. Do not make him go to the online

website to order if it is not necessary. Do not take the chance to lose the sale. Place the order for him, tell him about specials, free freight, volume discounts and anything else on sale that boost the value of the order. Never refuse to take an order while speaking with a customer.

550. **Offer The Password For Internet Access To Visitors Waiting Or Working On Company Premises:** Out of courtesy while the company visitors are waiting for meetings with company employees (i.e. vendors, customer representatives, maintenance service personnel, auditors), make sure the receptionist offers them access to the company's internet access so they may work on their laptop or their cell phone while waiting. They already may have it but offer it in case they are out of their own carrier's range.

551. **Insurance Certificates For All Vehicles Accessible To Drivers Via The Website:** Scan all the company vehicle insurance certificates to the company website for all

of the covered owned and rented cars, trucks, delivery vans, large trucks, trailers and all other units on wheels requiring registration. Give access to these current dated documents to all company drivers through an employee portal login on the company website and allow the documents to be downloaded and printed easily in the event a driver is out of state, missing the current certificate in the truck and needs to prove adequate insurance coverage. Always update the scans well ahead of the insurance cutoff deadline to give all drivers adequate notice to get their certificates printed to be carried in the cab.

552. **Verify Receipt Of All Rental Invoices For The Billed Period Before Payment In Accounts Payable:** Verify the receipt and current use of any rental unit (i.e. cars, trucks, trailers, plant equipment, mixers, compressors, etc.) before paying the invoices. Many companies rely on automatic invoicing. These bills are cut and mailed out sometimes without knowing if

those rented units were returned to the dealer or not (thus nullifying some or all the invoice charges). Many accounts payable invoices for rentals maybe charged to credit cards. The day that the invoice shows up and the credit card is charged (normally about two days later), verify the company is still renting the units and they are in possession of the rentals before paying the invoices. This is important because this is a temporary charge and can be stopped or returned at any time. Do not assume the employees who return the rented equipment, trucks, cars, etc. will notify accounts payable.

553. **Apply Cash Every Day To Find Out Payment Problems ASAP:** Watch the company bank account where deposits arrive and record those customer payments into the company's books (receivable accounts). Record all incoming cash (checks, ACHs, wire payments, lockbox deposits) every day. When applying these payments, notice the following issues: 1.)

missed invoices, 2.) debited or disputed charges deducted from customer payments, 3.) those companies incorrectly taking offered discounts outside the designated period (i.e. paying in 20 days and taking the discount when offered 1% 10, net 30 day terms), 4.) invoices skipped or missed because of price, quantity, quality problems or some other dispute.

554. **Perform These Checks Before Sending The First Invoice To A New Customer:** When preparing the first invoice to be sent to a customer, call ahead first and try to talk to the accounts payable person who will process the company invoice. If not yet received, request a state sales tax exemption certificate for that state where the sale occurred. Prepare the invoice and ensure pricing, units billed, freight costs, handling charges and any other billing amounts match those accepted by the customer's purchase order. Make sure the billing address is correct and that it is to be mailed or emailed or possibly entered into

an internet portal. If entered into a customer portal, your company billings clerk will need to be named, authorized, and given access to the customer's portal to enter new invoices. Once invoices are entered, the portal may yield to the reader the authorized payment date for the invoice that has been entered. Check to ensure the customer is paying on the same payment terms that the company bid was based. The portal could be different than the company quote, and it will need to be corrected as soon as possible before payment dates are scheduled to be made.

555. **Review Company Inventory Report Daily Or Weekly For Obvious Correctable Errors**: Run the company inventory report for glaring errors that need fixed on a regular basis: 1.) negative inventory balances (missing receivers to increase inventory, 2.) inventory balances in locations that are no longer used, 3.) inventory balances in wrong locations, 4.) inventory entered into incorrect part

numbers (from wrong purchase orders) , 5.)
inventory entered into incorrect categories
(stemming from incorrect purchase orders),
6.) invoicing not complete, 7.) receivers not
entered for received materials but billings
have been completed causing negative
balances, 8.) purchase order issued order
for parts at $1.00/each and vendor invoice
was issued and processed for $1.50/ each,
9.) items entered using wrong calendar
dates (sold before received into inventory).
These errors are avoidable if each
department and function followed the
company procedure (accounts payable
match invoice price to purchase order price,
receiving receive parts on correct date put
into inventory, keypunch entry verifies
inventory locations after entry, part number
corrections).

556. **Assign Drivers To Perform Routine
Inspections On Their Trucks Daily
Before Leaving:**   Assign the company
truck drivers to do an inspection daily on
their assigned truck or van to ensure 1.) oil

and fluid levels are adequate and correct, 2.) tires visually look full with no visible damage, cuts and no other hanging or loose truck parts not secure on the truck, 3.) motor sounds ok and not knocking or sputtering, 4.) time for scheduled maintenance has not lapsed, 5.) truck not carrying excess weight over permitted limits, 6.) no trouble lights visible on the dashboard, 7.) current insurance certificate is available inside the truck, 8.) current registration is available inside the truck, 9.) checklist of actions to take after an accident inside the truck, 10.) no brake noises or jerking when stopping noted, 11.) license plates and IFTA stickers current and securely on the truck, 12.) no other visible or known problems with the truck and 13.) full of gasoline/diesel or solar charged. This is a simple list and needs to be modified for every company given different circumstances and needs.

557. **Notify Customers Your Delivery Truck Is Running Late And Tell Them The**

New Time: Train all drivers to make deliveries ahead of schedule so that customers are normally happy and delighted that their shipment arrived early. When the shipment is known to be projected to run late (delays, service calls on equipment, delayed in traffic), require the driver to call back to his company's logistics contact to provide a new 'estimated time of arrival'. Have the inside salesperson call the customer quickly and notify him of the new estimated 'time of arrival' out of courtesy. Remember that this buyer may be waiting on the shipment to complete a production run and you have further stalled his production crew because they cannot finish because of your driver's schedule problems. Call him and keep him informed. Do not make the customer have to call you.

558. **Buy From Competitors And Find Out What You Are Not Doing Or Need To Improve:** Either buy products and services directly from your competitors or assign a

third party to do so in order to find out what your firm is not doing (or does not know how to do). Find out what other services the competition performs for customers. Study how their process differs (i.e. easier to order, faster delivery, better quality, better trained service personnel, longer warranty offered, more extensive detailed service performed, better trained onsite service personnel, excellent service record and instructions attached to the paid receipt, better follow-up on return trips, more options offered, more colors, more styles, better values for the money, two for one specials, discounts not offered elsewhere). Find out directly from the competitor why they excel or draw more sales than your company. Find out specifically what they do and do not do for their customers, where they lack experience all of which may offer future methods to compete.

559. **Reduce Purchases By Non-Purchasing Personnel:** Companies try to save money

by reducing the number of purchasing personnel which in the end, costs far more than having an additional purchasing agent calling for bids. The purchasing efforts of many employees at lower levels who rarely bid any assigned purchase end up spending far too much money. These inexperienced 'buyers' do not negotiate pricing, question vendors about charged sales taxes or control freight or delivery costs. They call one place to get the company worked on. They do not get competitive bids as they should. They contact a local supplies dealer and order what they need and have it delivered and never question the cost since accounts payable will pay for it. They make a call to order a service call to get a machine up and running without asking if there are any service agreements in place or if any parts were under warranty. They end up being expensive to companies when allowed to spend money. Do not allow non-purchasing personnel to make purchase decisions. Hire another skilled agent in

Purchasing and reassign purchasing tasks to those who can save the company money.

560. **Use SIC And NAICS Codes To Find Alternative Vendors**: Hire an intern (purchasing/business major in college) and give him a list of raw materials to call for and obtain price quotes. Look up the SIC codes or NAICS code of select current vendors and then run a listing of all the other companies assigned that same SIC or NACIS code within a radius of 100 miles, 200 miles (you pick the range). Rehearse with the intern the conversation he is to have with these potential vendors so he knows what to expect and specifics to request to obtain competitive prices (i.e. annual material usage estimate, price with freight and without, price volume discounts available, alternative cheaper products). Even though you may not buy from any of these quotes, you have exceptionally good market information, understand much more of the available market which will now help you to negotiate new pricing with your

current vendors. Once they hear you mention a few of their competitors' names, they will most likely be far more willing to negotiate better terms and prices versus losing your company's business.

561. **Forward Copies Of Your Company's Favorable Credit References To Those Good Customers**: Your customers will occasionally put your company down as a credit reference if they pay you well with no problems. When asked by outside companies to give credit references on some of those better customers, make sure to respond to these written requests as quickly as possible to help your customers, especially the fast paying ones. Help these preferred customers when you are able and, in this case, because they are good paying customers who pay on time, give them favorable reviews and forward them to their potential vendors through these requests. When finished, send a copy of your favorable comments and recommendation directly to those customers, and then email

or call them, tell them you responded favorably, offer to give more favorable reviews in the future and tell them you appreciate their business and all their timely payments. It is your way to reward their excellent payment history with your company.

562. **When Training New Employees, Restrict Overtime Until Fully Trained:** When the company hires new employees, they must be trained and during this training period, do not allow them to work overtime until finished. The employees are not fully productive and need to get fully trained and need to be motivated to learn as quickly as possible. If restricted from earning overtime premium, the new hire is far more likely to get through the training and prove himself to be allowed to work more hours.

563. **To Maximize Customer Visiting Time, Sort The Customers By Zip Code To Shorten Drive Times:** Assign sales visits in an organized manner where all the list of relevant customers are arranged in zip code

driving order. Minimize driving time between visits, maximize customer visit time where possible and mark those with the largest sales potential.

564. **Have Sales Personnel Drop Off Small Shipments – Meet Customers, Save Freight And Get Direct User Feedback**: Before the sales personnel take off on sales visits each day, instruct them to check the shipping department in order to pick up and deliver small shipments directly to customers. This gives them the opportunity to take the products directly to the customer's end user and original requestor behind the purchase order. When handing over the shipment, he can then ask for comments from the end users as to what they like and do not like and how else the company can improve products, add new products or help them also with product or service suggestions.

565. **Ask Machine Operators What Is Wrong Or Wasteful With The Machine Programming:** Many companies have

machine programmers which design the programming in manufacturing machines (i.e. laser cutters, grinders, EDM machines). The machine operators are the ones who know the errors with these programs (i.e. excess waste material, slow programming, slow reaction time). Ask them every day what they see wrong with the programmer's programs, especially on new or large manufacturing jobs where good productivity is extremely important.

566. **Are We Wasting Packaging Materials – Overwrapping and Over Banding?**
Shrink-wrap machines wrap plastic sheeting around products in boxes and other packages. There is normally a set number of wraps which is the maximum needed for shipping. Do your shipping personnel know what that maximum number of wraps is or has anyone posted the suggested number next to the machine? Ask your supplies representative the recommended maximum number of wraps for your company's machine so your

personnel are not over-wrapping all shipments going out of shipping. Banding around pieces of product are only needed to a specific number of bands and using more is pure waste and not worth the effort.

567. **When Calling To Confirm Receipt, Request The Number Counted And Received:** Sometimes in accounts payable a vendor will email their invoice and call and request their payment with a credit card or ACH wire. Verify the price and specifics of their invoice to your company's purchase order then call the department or facility that received the goods. Ask them to either prepare a receiver for you and send it or on the telephone to tell you that they received the items with no problems. At that point, ask them to declare the quantity that they counted. If they have not counted the goods, have them do so and call you back. Do not tell them the number invoiced to force them to acknowledge the correct number received. Normally they should prepare a receiving report to show

accounts payable personnel that the company did indeed receive the goods that were invoiced.

568. **Before Paying An Item On The Telephone Or The Internet, Search For A Coupon To Use:** When paying for an item on the telephone or directly on the internet, always look for a coupon to use first. Upon paying for your purchase, tell them you have a coupon to use and apply towards your purchase.

569. **Get Approval (In Writing) Before Paying An Invoice On The Telephone:** There will be times when a vendor will call and want paid for a new invoice. Before doing that, call and get approval on the telephone first from the person allowed to approve invoices. Do not allow the vendor to push for payment without getting internal approval. After calling, locating the approval person, and then getting them verbally to approve this payment, send an email in writing to confirm the approval, then cut the check or send the ACH wire.

570. **Never Tell Customers To Call Back –
Take Their Number And Get Sales To
Call Them:** When your employees take a
call and discover it is a customer asking
questions or one who needs help with
ordering, never tell them to call back.
Teach all employees to take a customer's
name and telephone number and tell them
someone will call them back quickly to
resolve their questions. Do not tell them to
call back at any future time or else you
teach them to call other more responsive
and responsible companies.

571. **Send Documents Via The Method The
Customer Requests:** If a customer asks
that invoices are to be emailed to an
address they provide, follow their
instructions. If a customer wants to call in
a telephone sales order, take their call and
then ask how they would like an
acknowledgement confirmation to be sent
or called back. If they fax in orders, call
them to confirm and ask how they want
documents returned to them. Do not try to

dictate to the customer if he resists because he will find another vendor that does what he wants.

572. **Get Internal Approval From Buyers Before Paying Invoices On The Telephone:** When a vendor calls in to ask for payment because your employee ordered a good or service (i.e. production is renting a machine, forklift, someone is buying material at a nearby store), request a copy of the invoice to be sent to you first. You need to check on prices, freight charged, handling charges, applicable sale taxes and anything else that is defined in the charges. There is either a purchase order or someone's written email to accounts payable which approves the payment. Ask for the purchase order and receiving report, or at best, get a written email describing what was ordered with price and quantity defined in the email for backup You need to know that the products, goods or services were truly

received and in good shape and in the quantity charged to the company.

573. **List All Vendor Auto-Debits And Request Their Supporting Invoices When Dollar Amounts Change:** Many companies now sign up for auto-debits which allows outside vendors to directly charge the company checking account for a repeating bill each month. If this is a mortgage payment with a known amortized amount each month, this would be understood and be booked normally without an invoice (fixed finance agreements charge the exact same dollar amount each month, covered in the original loan documents). Charges for any auto-debited charges though *that vary from month to month* should be accompanied by an invoice detailing the charges and showing what charges rose or dropped from the previous month (i.e. different kilowatts of electricity used for the month). Call the companies that auto-debit and request automatic emails of their invoices so they

can be checked for accuracy and correctness. Do not simply book auto-debits without getting approval or seeing the invoices. If you have an auto-debit for a monthly truck rental, the dollar amount will be the same, but you still need someone to verify the truck has not been returned. The rental rate should be different for the month that it is returned to the rental agency, thus this is the reason the guy renting the truck must tell either it was rented the whole month or the day it was returned (to match to the corresponding invoice).

574. **Tell Customers 'Sold-Out' Products Are Reordered And When They Are Arriving:** When a popular product is sold out, post a sign quickly and tell buyers seeking that product when your store's next shipment will arrive. Some customers may only shop for specific items at a store and are frustrated to go there only to see the product missing with no explanation. Do not make them go and seek out an employee who may not know when the

next shipment is coming in which further frustrates them. If you quickly post a clear sign at the product's normal shelf location that tells potential buyers the next shipment's arrival date: (examples: Product X will be here Friday afternoon, or "Coming Next Monday", "Product X arrives early on Saturday morning" or some other clear answer, they are more likely to return. Do not make them guess when your store will receive the next shipment or wonder if you are no longer stocking the item they want. Give them a specific date so they are not guessing.

575. **When Paying An Invoice Immediately, Ask If The Vendor Will Give A Cash Discount:** Sometimes the company must pay for goods or services upfront at the time of the sale (versus extended credit). The company will either pay the invoice by wire, manual check or by credit card. At that point before sending the total amount, ask for a cash discount and see if the vendor will allow it to be deducted from the

wired payment (i.e. 1% or 1 ½% or 2%). If true, make the argument since they offer an early payment discount to credit customers, yours should be able to take a discount given that you were not given any credit terms.

576. **When A Customer States They Do Not Issue Written Formal Purchase Orders, Create A Legal One With Your Return Email**:   When a customer calls and orders goods or services without issuing a purchase order with their order, respond to them via email with the company's acceptance of their offer detailing their stated order quantity to be shipped, accepted piece price, agreed upon freight terms, applicable sales tax, buyer's name, shipment due date, buyer's contact telephone number and the correct ship to address where the goods are going. Include any other chargeable items that are related to the shipment. Once this is created, send it to the person who sent in the order and ask them to accept your email (acceptable

purchase order substitute). Your agreement in writing suffices the necessary requirements to go to court.

577. **Do Not Hire Employees, Then Lay Them Off And Pay Them Through AP:** Unless an ex-employee starts a business and obtains a Federal tax identification number, do not hire ex-employees through accounts payable after you have terminated them. They will get a W2 from the company under their social security number then get theoretically receive from you one of the types of form 1099 from your company for the payments you made to them as contractors through the purchasing department (with none of the employer mandated employment taxes). This will raise a red flag to the IRS and may be considered tax fraud on the company's behalf when it seems from both tax forms to be avoiding all of the required employer taxes (matching FICA tax, federal unemployment tax (FUTA), state unemployment tax (SUTA), worker's

compensation insurance required for all employees under their correct work classifications, etc.

578. **Do Not Issue Accounts Payable Checks To People Or Companies Without Addresses On The Checks:** When paying your vendors in accounts payable, you are responsible to get a signed and dated W9 from them which declares their social security number or their assigned federal identification number, thus the checks that you cut for them should always have a current address for them. Your company should not issue checks with physical address printed on the check. It also helps them to cash them check when asked for identification and it matches the check.

579. **Send Emails To Potential Customer Buyers' Just Before A Holiday And You Will Get Names Of Secondary Buyers**: If you want to obtain as many people's names in customers' purchasing departments, send the main buyers an email just before a major holiday and you will

receive an automated email back announcing they are out of the office but the following named personnel are handling incoming issues during these holidays. Those names provided are normally the secondary personnel in the buyer's office who your salespeople need to know, especially in the future event a buyer leaves a customer's firm. Make it a point to gather up as much information about all the buyers of your customers and enter all of it into your database. They can be included in mass emails, specials and other marketing events or sales your firm is holding.

580. **Always Pay Employees Correctly, And If Necessary, Spend Extra To Pay Them On Time**: Regardless of the reasons that caused payroll delays, always pay company employees on time. If a commission amount was not calculated until the 15th and payroll was due on the 15th, wire the net paycheck so the recipient gets it the same day into his checking account at his

bank. If an employee is short paid due to various supervisor or payroll department errors, offer to cut the check or wire the difference to the employee same day. The employee should always know they will be paid on time by the company.

581. **Plan Payroll To Be Paid Two Days Before The Employees' Pay Date:** Most companies hire outside payroll companies to run payroll calculations, deduct all the required taxes and then issue payroll checks to all the company employees. Companies hire these payroll firms because they do not have or want to invest in the necessary legal resources to keep up with all various city, county, and state tax changes. In order for these payroll companies to pay payroll and taxes on time, they must normally be paid first by your company. That normally will happen two business days prior to the pay date. This is required because they will debit your bank account and will wait 24 hours to ensure your company does not dispute and reverse the debit, then they will

issue your employees their paychecks and automatic deposits. They want to ensure they are not denied getting paid by the banking system and companies can reverse these debits for a limited time. Plan for all payroll expense to occur two days before payroll dates because of this banking issue.

582. **How Long Does It Take To Change Screens On The Company Website?** One of the main complaints about internet websites is how slow they are. If your company website requires more than a few seconds to change screens for visitors, they will not return to the website. Ask your website maintenance company to speed up the company website and if they cannot, hire another firm to do it. You want visitors to come online so do not chase them away with poor and incompetent programming.

583. **How Long To Issue Financial Statements? Shorten The Process To Make Decisions**: Give instructions to accounting to close the company's financial records as early as possible in order for the

previous month's results can be reviewed and analyzed quickly to make management decisions (i.e. hire more sales personnel, layoff excessive employees, curtail overtime, reduce spending, place certain overstocked products on sale, raise prices on specific losing product lines, curtail excessive travel expenses, analyze sales by representative, industry, regions, customer and any other relevant measurements). Tell accounting to accrue reasonable costs that are yet to be received to get the books closed versus waiting forever for the last invoice. Assuming the company forces all buyers to use a purchase order system (which records all purchases and liabilities with agreed upon price and quantity estimates), accrue all of the received purchase orders that are missing invoices from the vendors, so the costs hit the correct month. The financial results will not be perfect but managers who truly run the company never need perfect numbers to see glaring favorable or unfavorable trends.

They normally do not have the luxury of unlimited time to make decisions.

584. **Post All Late Jobs On A Large TV Screen Above The Shipping Office:** Have your IT person install a large screen in the shipping department to show all employees the past due orders with the worst at the top of the list (yes, like the drive-thru at the fast food restaurant). Make the screen large enough to easily read and key into the database completed shipments asap so the list updates and shows the next important past due shipment that needs attention. The screen should show the customer name, order number, original due date and most importantly the number of days the shipment is currently late. This large screen has the same function as the computer monitor inside the restaurant indicating the next order due to the car sitting in the drive-through lane outside the fast-food restaurant window. Make the screen current by keeping orders current. You may want to add a field next

to each order as to the status of the order (i.e. "in progress", "material on order, due tomorrow"). Teach all employees to understand the screen, learn the importance of finishing orders in order of importance and how to update the list. Their goal in shipping should be to have no orders late (except those waiting on outside material which is controlled by purchasing personnel).

585. **Pay Shipping Employees To Reduce / Eliminate Late Jobs: Pay Them To Ship Early**: Consider establishing a bonus program for all the shipping personnel that is based upon getting out shipments by established due dates or promise dates. Subtract from the payout for wrong shipments, returned goods not ordered, improperly packaged items, etc.

586. **Ask For Expediting Fees If Customers Call And Need Faster Delivery**: A company incurs cost when an order is required to be sped up and sent out earlier than normal. Customers fully realize their

demands cost money so most are prepared to pay for these additional costs. Make sure to tell these customers who want expedited service what they will be paying for the service prior to starting the job and ask the customer to acknowledge the additional fees before incurring them. Costs for production rise because normal jobs are sometimes delayed or put off to the side to allow another to be completed first. This causes an increase in payroll, more expensive freight for delivery, a change in the company's production timeline and scheduler changes to meet the demands of the customer. Make sure a premium is charged for this service.

587. **Instruct All Drivers To Send Pictures Of Signed BOLS (Bills Of Lading) To Billings <u>Before </u>Leaving Customers' Sites:** When your driver delivers goods to a company, after the customer's employee counts and verifies all received goods, he will normally ask for the receiving department personnel to sign and date the

bill of lading to acknowledge the receipt of goods. That bill of lading may also state the arrival and departure times which captures potential demurrage (time above agreed upon delivery or pickup time hour estimate). Instruct the driver (your employee or contractor) to take a picture of this signed document and send it to your company's billings department so the delivery can be billed immediately. If a freight company is hired to do the delivery, require the signed BOL to be sent at the time of leaving the customer's site and not several days later.

588. **Require Outside Freight Companies To Send Signed BOLS Immediately After Customer Delivery:** Many hired freight companies will wait and send the signed BOL with their invoice which may not be received for a week or more into the company's accounts payable department. Mandate in the terms of the purchase orders to all outside freight companies that their assigned drivers will take and send pictures

of the signed bills of lading (BOLs) to the company's billings person upon leaving the customer's site with no delay. Give the email address of the billings contact for the company to all hired freight companies in order that this backup document is provided as early as possible to expedite billing. Most customers want proofs of delivery accompanying the initial invoice, so billing is dependent upon having this backup to forward with the invoice.

589. **Bill Sales Immediately – Some Online Invoicing Portals Are Designed To Delay Payments:** Bill customers as quickly as possible because many of the new online invoicing portals will not allow backdating invoices which moves ultimate payment dates forward. For example, a company truck delivers to a customer on a Monday (6/1), the driver delays and sends a picture of the bill of lading on Wednesday (6/3) to billings. The billings person receives the paperwork and then creates and enters the invoice into the customer's billing portal

online on Thursday (6/4). That portal may or may not allow backdating the invoice back to the correct Monday date when the actual delivery and technical sale occurred. It may date the invoice as of the date the invoice was entered into the portal. That could delay payment later than normal. If the agreed upon payment terms were net 10, the company which delivered the goods now will most likely not be paid until the 13th or 14th day. If the vendor only pays invoices once per week, it could be worse especially if paid by a check in the mail which adds several days. Eliminate all possible delays in billings.

590. **Talk To Incoming Truck Drivers And Ask What Is Wrong / Unorganized / Delayed Or Needs Improvement:** Take the time to offer something to drink or the use of the company's restroom for arriving truck drivers bringing materials and supplies to your company. If you ask them, they may discuss the locations where they just delivered, which companies are the

best organized or easiest to deliver or unload, which customers are the worst and most unorganized, which seem the busiest and which have noticeably far few employees remaining. Ask them what problems do they have with your company when they come to unload and what could the company do to make the delivery easier? Truck drivers are rarely asked anything so they will most likely be happy to share ideas that can be used to speed up the company's internal process. They see many examples of companies that operate better and worse than your firm so ask and listen. Remember that some of the them work directly for your customers so treat them well.

591. **Always Get An Outside Quote When A Vendor Offers Internal Financing Options:** When making a large purchase from a vendor (i.e. machinery, AC units, grinder, large truck, water pollution system, electrical system, etc.) who offers an associated financing company to finance

the purchase, always take and review the offer and then make sure to get an outside second financing bid based on the same quote and period of financing. If that second bid comes in at a lower cost than the vendor's associated financing company's offer, go back to the vendor, tell them his financing company is too high and ask him to have them revisit their bid since they will lose the business. Do this through the vendor and not through the financing firm. Try to negotiate and use the vendor's financing option if possible because the sale will execute more quickly not involving outside firms. But if pricing is too high, tell the vendor his option is too costly and choose the outside financing option. Most of the time the vendor will help you by putting pressure on its financing associate, and that firm will drop its price to match the competition in order not to lose the sale. Remember that in exchange for referring customers to their financing option, vendors normally are paid a referral fee, so there is almost always room in the original bid. The main reason to negotiate through the vendor is that he will not want to be associated with more expensive financing and will put almost always put pressure on their associated financing company.

592. **Most Company Payrolls Are Too Complicated, Pay An Outside Service To Avoid Fines / Penalties**: Most companies hire outside payroll companies to run payroll calculations, deduct all the required taxes, file taxes and deduct and pay on time all other mandated employee deductions and then issue payroll checks to all the company employees. Companies hire this service because they do not have the internal resources to keep up with tax changes. If your company has multiple sites and lots of employees, do not risk fines and penalties trying to do the payroll internally. Your firm most likely does not have the resources to handle all the tax deadlines, due dates, and other technical issues. It risks being fined if taxes are filed

incorrectly or late or if your firm misses court ordered garnishments for child support, court ordered fines to be payroll deducted or any other of hundreds of possibilities. Taxes are different in cities, counties, and all states. Hire a reputable outside firm. Almost any of them can do a better job than your company. Payroll is all they do.

593. **After A Land Or Building Purchase, Check County Property Tax Records Online:** After any sale or purchase of property (i.e. land, buildings, vehicles, equipment) go to the county tax assessor's property tax website to check on assigned appraised values, tax calculations and correct owners' names: Once your company buys a piece of property, you need to check to ensure the name on the property is changed at the county tax appraisal's office. If you are a homeowner, you will want to check to make sure the name changes so you can claim a homestead exemption for reducing the

property taxes (that cannot happen if the old owner remains the owner on record). If you are a business, you want to check the assigned appraised value of the property to ensure it is not overvalued above your purchase price, otherwise you will need to protest the price. You also want to ensure once you have sold a piece of property that it comes off your name, especially at the tax yearend so you do not have to fight a tax bill that is not yours on the last day of the tax year. Check to make sure the owner's name has been changed and the new owner's name and mailing address is correct (property address and mailing address may be different if owning multiple properties).

594. **Take Any Type Of Tax Payment (Checks) To The Post Office And Send Certified Mail:** Assuming you do not want to wire a payment, you can mail your payments and enjoy a delay in them clearing your bank for a few days. In order to ensure your firm can prove they paid

their taxes if they pay taxes by manual checks (i.e. estimated state taxes, franchise taxes, property taxes), go and send those checks at the post office and send them certified mail to ensure they are sent and received. Pay for the "return to sender card" (green) which will come back to you signed by the recipient's agent once the checks are delivered. The post office stamped date proves you paid the taxes on time and the certified mail ensures they must sign for the check received. The returned card sent back to you shows proof if necessary that your taxes were paid on time and that they received them (or someone at that address received them). Some companies wire funds to pay taxes but many small companies mail payments (to gain time from mail delay).

595. **Mark Your Building With The Physical Address – Make It Easy To Find Your Business:** Put numbers on the front of your building and add the street name also if you like. Make it easy for anyone to find

you: delivery men, customers, vendors. Make sure your name and the street number are both easy to spot from the street for someone coming to your business the first time. People question why a business has neither their name on the building let alone forgetting to add their correct address. Make it easy for anyone to find you to come do business.

596. **Always Send Proofs Of Delivery With All Invoices:** When billing customers, automatically send the proof of delivery (signed clearly and dated bill of lading indicating someone in their receiving department signed for your shipment). Whenever sending a copy of a missed invoice to a customer, always attach a proof of delivery along with the invoice because if they are missing the invoice, they will ask for it anyway. Make it easy for them to pay you as soon as possible.

597. **Publish A List Of All Businesses' Discounts In Your Zip Code And Pass Them Out Free:** Hire an intern to

assemble a listing of all businesses within your zip code. Have him call them and ask them what they sell, service and their telephone number and hours of operation. Put this into a book sorted by business category, get it printed with as many copies as there are businesses and then give copies to your sales personnel. Assign them to visit customers and give out these business listings free and encourage neighbor businesses to offer others in the manual discounts on products and services since the freight is cheaper and those customers nearby are more easily serviced than those customers far away. Print several hundred more copies of these business listings to have in the lobby, to give out by purchasing personnel to encourage buying within the zip code, to give out by delivery drivers in the local area and most importantly distributed freely to neighboring companies by the company's inside and outside sales personnel. Make sure to put your company's name, telephone number and your offered discount to all these local businesses. Put a person's name as a main contact to take inquiries.

598. **Offer To Open Your Facility Early For Hired Freight Haulers In Exchange For A Discount:** Most of the time when companies hire freight companies to come and haul goods or materials to another location, the hired trucks show up the night before or much earlier than the normal company opening time. Many times, they are sitting in the parking lot waiting for the first person to open the building. Most truck drivers would like to load up as early as possible to get on the road, get to their destination and finish the job to enable them to take additional paid freight loads. Allowing them to get loaded or unloaded earlier than normal may be worth it to them if offered ahead of schedule to give up a freight discount. Explain to them the discount will pay for the overtime for the employees asked to come in early and open the facility to load or unload the truck. Some truckers will accept, and some will

not if they are not busy with other paid trip options. For some, it may be worth it to gain two or three hours in driving for the day so ask if they are interested. It will help speed up production, free up a busy receiving dock and will pay some willing employees justified overtime to come in a few hours early.

599. **For Credit Card Payments, Offer A Small Bonus To Check Personal ID And Cut Store Theft**: Companies take credit cards and rarely ask for a form of the person's personal identification. To reduce the rate of theft that the store incurs, ask the customer for a piece of personal identification (i.e. picture I.D., picture driver's license, Passport with photo). In exchange, offer a small discount cut from the bill total. Most honest customers will be glad to offer the identification to cut the bill total, even for a small amount. Those who do not want the cut may use another form of payment (especially those who do not have any photo ID to back up the stolen

card). Stolen cards are hard to use if one must present a personal ID with picture on it.

600. **Expand Sales - Have Your Inside Sales Personnel Sell Goods & Services Outside The Company Catalog**: When a company has inside sales personnel who are knowledgeable and are well respected by their customers, consider expanding what they can sell to their customers including lots of items not carried by the company. Some customer buyers do not have the time to find everything so they will depend upon an inside salesperson who they trust to go find goods and services for them. Tell your inside sales personnel to let their customers know that they can buy nearly anything else (off the shelf) that needs to be bought to ease the burden on the buyer. Make up a list of items that are not offered directly by the company and make customers know about the expanded capabilities of these inside sales representatives. Examples: 1.) an appliance store that also offers electrical

wiring contractors to run wiring for more appliances (third party), 2.) supermarket that can arrange catering services, 3.) seamstress who can offer outside clothing selection services, 4.) metal manufacturing company that also arranges painting, finishing, plating and metal assembly and packaging if necessary, 5.) manufacturing supplies representative who can also arrange some contractor services (i.e. electrical wiring, AC/DC work, remodeling kitchens and bathrooms).

My Favorite Ideas

My Favorite Ideas

_____

_____

_____

_____

_____

_____

_____

_____

_____

_____

_____

_____

_____

_____

_____

_____

_____

_____

_____

_____

_____

_____

My Favorite Ideas

My Favorite Ideas

_____
_____
_____
_____
_____
_____
_____
_____
_____
_____
_____
_____
_____
_____
_____
_____
_____
_____
_____
_____
_____
_____
_____

My Favorite Ideas

_____

_____

_____

_____

_____

_____

_____

_____

_____

_____

_____

_____

_____

_____

_____

_____

_____

_____

_____

_____

_____

_____

My Favorite Ideas

My Favorite Ideas

_____
_____
_____
_____
_____
_____
_____
_____
_____
_____
_____
_____
_____
_____
_____
_____
_____
_____
_____
_____
_____
_____
_____
_____

My Favorite Ideas

My Favorite Ideas